BLOCKCHAIN

Bitcoin and Ethereum

By Sam Sutton

~~~

BITCOIN

Mastering Bitcoin for Starters

By Sam Sutton
~~~

© Copyright 2018 By Sam Sutton
All Rights Reserved

The transmission, duplication or reproduction of any of the following work including specific information will be considered an illegal act irrespective of if it is done electronically or in print. This extends to creating a secondary or tertiary copy of the work or a recorded copy and is only allowed with express written consent from the Publisher. All additional right reserved.

The information in the following pages is broadly considered to be a truthful and accurate account of facts and as such any inattention, use or misuse of the information in question by the reader will render any resulting actions solely under their purview. There are no scenarios in which the publisher or the original author of this work can be in any fashion deemed liable for any hardship or damages that may befall them after undertaking information described herein. This book should not be taken as financial or investment advice, and the author does not take any responsibility for inaccuracies, omissions, or errors which may be found therein.

Additionally, the information in the following pages is intended only for informational purposes and should thus be thought of as universal. As befitting its nature, it is presented without assurance regarding its prolonged validity or interim quality. Trademarks that are mentioned are done without written consent and can in no way be considered an endorsement from the trademark holder.

The contents of this book are intended to convey general information only. You should not treat any information herein as a call to make any particular decision regarding cryptocurrency usage, legal matters, investments, taxes, cryptocurrency mining, exchange usage, wallet usage, etc. It is strongly suggested that you seek advice from your own financial, investment, tax, or legal adviser. This book should not be taken as financial or investment advice, and the author does not take any responsibility for inaccuracies, omissions, or errors. The author of this work is not responsible for any loss, damage, or inconvenience caused as a result of reliance on information as published on, or linked to, this book.

The author of this book has taken careful measures to share vital information about the subject. May its readers acquire the right knowledge, wisdom, inspiration, and succeed.

TABLE OF CONTENTS

Introduction 7

Chapter 1: What is Bitcoin? 9

Chapter 2: Getting Started with Bitcoin 17

Chapter 3: Understanding Blockchain and
Bitcoin Transactions 19

Chapter 4: Where to Keep Your Bitcoin 23

Chapter 5: Buying Bitcoin 27

Chapter 6: Using Bitcoin 31

Chapter 7: Investing in Bitcoin 33

Chapter 8: Bitcoin for Business 39

Chapter 9: Bitcoin mining 41

Chapter 10: Security of Bitcoin 45

Conclusion 47

SAM SUTTON

INTRODUCTION

Congratulations on downloading this book and thank you for doing so.

The following chapters will teach you the ins and outs of investing in bitcoin and how you can turn it into a goldmine of profits:

Chapter 1 lays down the basics to help you to have a good understanding of what bitcoin really is.

Chapter 2 gives an overview and teaches how you can get started with using bitcoin.

Chapter 3 discusses the blockchain technology which is the backbone technology of bitcoin. It also explains how a bitcoin transaction works.

Chapter 4 talks about the different types of bitcoin wallets.

Chapter 5 teaches how you can buy bitcoins.

Chapter 6 is about using bitcoin. Learn about receiving, sending, and receiving bitcoins.

Chapter 7 teaches effective strategies that you can use to invest in bitcoin.

Chapter 8 talks about businesses that use bitcoins, as well as how *you* can easily use it for your own business.

Chapter 9 is about bitcoin mining. Learn about the different ways to mine bitcoins.

Chapter 10 talks about the security of using bitcoin.

There are plenty of books on this subject on the market, thanks again for choosing this one! Every effort was made to ensure it is full of as much useful information as possible. Please enjoy!

CHAPTER 1:
WHAT IS BITCOIN?

Bitcoin is undeniably the number one cryptocurrency in the world. What is a *cryptocurrency*? A cryptocurrency is a kind of digital asset that is held electronically. It is stored online; and therefore, it does not have a physical existence. Just like other cryptocurrencies, bitcoin functions as a substitute for money.

Bitcoin is a *decentralized* digital currency. It is decentralized in the sense that there is no government, organization, group, or person that exercises authority over it. This makes it free from any and all forms of manipulation and undue advantage. This is also why so many people trust bitcoin.

It should be noted that although cryptocurrencies like bitcoin work as a substitute for money, they are not considered as fiat money or legal tender. Fiat money refers to the established and official currency of a state such as the US dollar. Legal tender refers to "that which a debtor may compel a creditor to accept payment." Although bitcoin is not considered as fiat money or legal tender, it is noteworthy that many individuals and merchants these days now accept bitcoin as a medium of payment. In fact, among all the cryptocurrencies out there, bitcoin is the most accepted cryptocurrency. Just to give you an idea, the giant computer company, Microsoft, now accepts payments in bitcoins. Not only that, Virgin Galactic, a huge company engaged in space tourism, also accepts payments in bitcoins. Other known companies like Overstock, Fiverr, Steam, Peach Airlines, Lionsgate Films, and Stripe, among many others, accept and use bitcoins. As Bitcoin gets more and more popular in the market, the more people and businesses start to use it.

Brief History

In 2008, a paper was posted on a cryptography mailing list. It was entitled *Bitcoin: A Peer-to-Peer Electronic Cash System*. It was published under the name Satoshi Nakamoto, which turned out to be just a pseudonym. The following year, Bitcoin was finally launched in the market. It came into existence just after Nakamoto himself mined the very first bitcoin block known as the *genesis block*.

Back then, bitcoin did not have any significant value. In fact, so many people did not even realize how much bitcoin would grow. At that time, it was the members of the cryptocurrency community themselves who decided how much bitcoin would worth. For example, there was a famous transaction where two pizzas where bought for 10,000 bitcoins. This is still posted on the *bitcointalk* forum. As you can see, most of the people there did not take it seriously. If only they knew how much bitcoin would develop. As of January 16, 2018, the price of 1 bitcoin is around 13,500 USD.

Who is Satoshi Nakamoto?

When people talk about the creator of bitcoin, they are well aware that it was made by Satoshi Nakamoto. But, who exactly is Satoshi Nakamoto? The truth is that up to the present time, nobody knows the real identity of Satoshi Nakamoto. There are many different views about this: There are those who say that Nakamoto is actually composed of a group of computer experts and programmers, while others say that Nakamoto is even a woman. Another theory is that Satoshi Nakamoto is Hal Finney, the man who first downloaded the bitcoin software and received 10 bitcoins from Nakamoto simply for downloading it. However, when Mr. Finney was still alive, he had already denied this claim. It is also worth mentioning that *Satoshi* is also the smallest unit of bitcoin. Bitcoin has 8 decimal places. Example: $0.00000001 = 1$ satoshi. Simply put, no one knows for certain the true identity of Satoshi Nakamoto. Nakamoto has long withdrawn from the public that nobody even knows his whereabouts. However, even though nobody knows who the real Satoshi Nakamoto is, and even if his identity remains a mystery forever, the fruit of his labor and contribution to the world, bitcoin, has gained worldwide popularity and success.

Why Invest in Bitcoin?

It is not a secret that most people who engage in the cryptocurrency market and possess bitcoins do not really use such cryptocurrency as a mere medium of exchange. In fact, they view bitcoin as a form of investment. So, you must be thinking: *Just how much profit can I reasonably make?* To give you an idea, here is the classic example: If you had invested even just $500 in bitcoin in 2009 or even in 2010, then you would have already earned millions by now. Yes, this is how profitable investing in bitcoin can be. Unlike investing in stocks where an annual return of 30% is already considered very high, you can obviously earn so much more when you invest in bitcoin. Hence, many professional stock investors have started moving their investments from stocks into bitcoins. Another benefit of investing in bitcoin is that you do not have to wait for a year just to experience a significant price increase. It is not uncommon for the price of bitcoin to increase by more than 30% within a week. There was even a time when the price of bitcoin increased by $2,000 in just a week's time.

Investing in bitcoin is also easy and convenient. Since cryptocurrencies are held electronically online, all you need is Internet access to start investing, and you can manage your account and all your investments in the comfort of your home. In fact, you can even do all these directly from your mobile phone. Indeed, now is the time for you to enjoy the beauty of technology and the profitability of bitcoin.

Of course, just like any other investment, there is also a risk that you may not earn anything and that you may even lose your investment. However, there are strategies that you can do to prevent this from happening. By using the right strategies as revealed in this book, you can effectively increase your rate of success by more than 75%.

So, should you invest in bitcoin? Well, if you are the type who is afraid of taking risks, then perhaps this investment is not right for you. However, if you are the type who wants to earn and enjoy a high amount of profit, if you are willing to take risks and spend time and effort to study the market, if you want a proven way to achieve financial freedom, then investing in bitcoin might just be the best investment decision that you can ever make.

High Volatility

When people talk about bitcoin, they usually say that it has a high volatility. This is true. But, what does it mean when you say that bitcoin has a *high volatility*? This means that the price of bitcoin changes rapidly and significantly. This explains why it is possible for you to earn more than 200% profit in just a few days. However, be careful about this since this also implies that it is also possible for the price of bitcoin to drop just as fast. This is a normal part of the risk of investing in bitcoin or any other cryptocurrency. The whole cryptocurrency market itself is simply highly volatile. However, do not let this discourage you. Just remember that it is exactly this high volatility nature of bitcoin that makes it a highly lucrative investment. The good news is that if you study the past and current trend of bitcoin, you can easily see that it is a very profitable investment. Indeed, the price of bitcoin as of the beginning of 2018 has been gradually decreasing. However, keep in mind that it first increased significantly. This is merely part of the usual fluctuations that you can expect in the market. The important thing is that, in the long run, the value of your investment should be growing. Bitcoin has well established itself for years, and nobody can deny that it is still the number one and most successful cryptocurrency in the market.

Be careful with your understanding of high volatility. Many people think that high volatility means that after a significant price increase, then the price will drop significantly afterward, and vice versa, as if it balancing the rise and fall of the price on its own. This is a wrong understanding of high volatility. Take note that bitcoin (as well as other cryptocurrencies) does not balance itself on its own. Instead, some factors affect its price, such as market competition, economy, technological developments, market acceptance, and government regulations, among many others. Hence, you need to consider all these factors when predicting whether the price of bitcoin will rise or fall, but rest assured that a cryptocurrency will not balance its price movements all by itself. This is also why you need to do research and analysis when you engage in the cryptocurrency market.

What are Altcoins?

When you read about bitcoin, you will definitely also encounter other cryptocurrencies like Ethereum, Litecoin, Ripple, Lisk, OmiseGO, and others. All of these are altcoins. Simply put, all cryptocurrencies are considered as altcoin except bitcoin. Bitcoin has established itself strongly in the market that it has become the leading standard of all cryptocurrencies, such that all other coins are merely called as *altcoins*, a term that is simply short for *alternative coins*. To date, there are already more than 1,000 altcoins that have been created. Still, among all the cryptocurrencies in the world, Bitcoin holds the number one position and is considered the top and most successful and popular cryptocurrency of all.

Anonymity

Bitcoin users enjoy a certain level of anonymity. This is because, in a bitcoin transaction, no personal details will be revealed. This is true even though bitcoin has a *public* blockchain. When you look at the bitcoin blockchain, you will only see a bitcoin wallet address of the sender and of the bitcoin wallet address of the recipient. You will also see the amount of bitcoins involved in the transaction, as well as a time stamp. However, the names and other sensitive information will remain confidential. What about the bitcoin wallet address? It is simply like a long string of random letters and numbers, and a bitcoin user can always request for a new wallet address for free with just a few clicks of a mouse. In fact, it is suggested that to minimize exposure, you should request for a new wallet address for every new transaction that you make.

On legal matters

Although bitcoin is decentralized in such a way that no central authority governs and controls it, it does not mean that states do not have the power to regulate its use within their jurisdiction. Due to the level of anonymity enjoyed by bitcoin users, it is not hard to understand why some states like Ecuador and Bolivia completely outlaw the use of bitcoins, as well as all other cryptocurrencies. Due to the nature of cryptocurrencies, they can easily be used in illegal activities like money laundering and tax evasion. The good news is that in many countries like in the U.S., Canada, Europe, Russia, South Korea, Singapore, Philippines, and so many others, the use of bitcoins and other cryptocurrencies is legal. Russia used to consider it as illegal but then it changed its position in 2017 and now also uses bitcoin. Over time, more and more states and businesses are being open to the use of bitcoin.

As a bitcoin investor, you should keep an eye on the latest government regulations on bitcoin and other cryptocurrencies. Although there are states that do not outlaw the use of bitcoin in their territories, it does not mean that they can no longer impose regulations on the use of bitcoin. As of recently, the price of bitcoin and other known cryptocurrencies have been experiencing a decline. According to the news, this is because of certain regulations imposed by various states. But, do not worry; this has always been expected to happen. This is just one of the fluctuations that you can expect in the market. Soon enough, things will get more stable, and you can expect the prices to increase again. One thing to remember is that legal matters, especially the regulations imposed by states, have a strong influence on the price of bitcoin, as well as other cryptocurrencies. For example, when a news piece was released stating that South Korea was considering shutting down all its cryptocurrency exchanges, the price of bitcoin and all other cryptocurrencies experienced a significant decrease in price. This is nothing new; back in 2017, China also made a similar declaration, and the price of bitcoin and altcoins also experienced a drop in price. Once again, the lesson here is to consider how governments react to the use of cryptocurrencies, especially with regard to their legalities.

CHAPTER 2:
GETTING STARTED WITH BITCOIN

Now that you have a good idea of what bitcoin is, it is time for you to have an overview of how to get started with bitcoin so that you will know just what to expect. Well, the first step is to create a bitcoin wallet. There are basically just two types of bitcoin wallets: The hot and cold wallet. However, they are further divided into more specific types. Do not worry; they will be discussed in detail later on in this book. For now, you should learn what hot and cold wallets are.

Simply put, a hot wallet is a kind of bitcoin wallet that is stored completely online. As such, it is very easy and convenient to use. Hence, most cryptocurrency users use a hot wallet. All that you need to do is to sign up for an account for free from a wallet provider like *Coinbase*. The signing up process usually takes less than two minutes to complete. After which, you can now start using your bitcoin wallet. A cold wallet is the kind of bitcoin wallet where you store your private and public keys *offline*. Hence, to access your wallet and transfer funds, you will need to have your cold wallet in your possession. This is an added and highly effective security measure.

The next step is for you to own bitcoins. After all, the only way to invest and take advantage of bitcoin is by having bitcoins of your own. Although there are different ways to earn bitcoins, the quickest and fastest way to earn a good amount of bitcoins is by buying them. Bitcoin wallets like Coinbase will allow you to buy (and even sell) bitcoins directly from the wallet itself. This makes things very convenient for you. However, if the wallet that you use does not allow you to buy bitcoins, then you can simply sign up for a trading account with a cryptocurrency trading broker.

Again, creating an account is also fast and simple. However, it is important that you only work with a reliable and trusted broker. When you search online, you will surely find different brokers. As an investor, it is important that you only work with a reliable broker, so be sure to check the latest ratings and reviews of a broker prior to making any form of deposit.

Once you have bitcoins of your own, then you can keep them, and then sell them at a profit once they appreciate in value. However, the activity of investing in bitcoin is much more technical than just buying and selling bitcoin. After all, how do you know the right time to buy and sell bitcoin? Do not worry; all these will be discussed later in the book. For now, it is important for you to just have an idea of how you will get started.

As a bitcoin investor, you should know that research and analysis should be part of your day-to-day activity as an investor. Hence, before you even start to actually use and invest in bitcoin, you should already begin reading about the cryptocurrency market by now. Take note that bitcoin has many other competitors. Therefore, even though you may only intend to invest in bitcoin, it is still important that you keep an eye on its competitors, such as Ethereum, Litecoin, Ripple, Dash, and others. And, who knows, you might even be able to discover other profitable investment opportunities in the process.

CHAPTER 3:
UNDERSTANDING BLOCKCHAIN AND BITCOIN TRANSACTIONS

Before we discuss the specific steps on how you can profit by investing in bitcoin, you should first understand the technology behind bitcoin. Take note that the backbone technology of bitcoin is known as the *blockchain technology* or simply *blockchain*. What is blockchain? It is a public and decentralized distributed ledger which also acts as a repository of all transactions. It is made of records referred to as blocks. Before any block is added to the chain, it will undergo a strict process of verification and confirmation, which ensures that all the records that will be added to the chain are true and correct. Every new block is connected to the block that comes before it using what is known as a *hash pointer*. This way, all of the blocks in the blockchain network are interconnected with one another.

The blockchain is decentralized, which means that no organization exercises authority over it. It functions on its own free from any and all forms of influence and manipulation. This is why many people trust this system since there is no need for human intervention and control. The blockchain is also public, which means that all of the transactions are viewable to everyone on the network. This gives it added transparency and fairness and ensures that all transactions are legitimate and correct.

The blockchain technology is also an effective preventive measure against double spending and fraud, which are common problems in financial circles. When you use blockchain, there is absolutely no way to withdraw, modify, or cancel a transaction after it is confirmed. Not even Satoshi Nakamoto himself can stop or change it.

It also has a high level of security. Keep in mind that the blockchain network is spread over a wide connection of computers. For an attack against the blockchain system to be successful, the said attack has to possess at least 51% of the total hash rate of the entire bitcoin blockchain. Since the network is spread over a vast number of computers, achieving the said 51% can be considered as impossible. Take note that an attack with less than 51% hash rate is still possible, but you simply cannot expect for it to be successful. This is the idea behind the 51% attack concept.

It is noteworthy that bitcoin is not the only one that is gaining lots of attention and popularity. The blockchain technology has been making a name for itself apart from it being associated with bitcoin and other cryptocurrencies. This is because the blockchain has many other possible applications that are even well beyond the financial sector. Still, it can be said that blockchain is still a fairly new and young technology. Hence, there is still a room for improvement, and it is definitely something to keep an eye on.

How a Bitcoin Transaction Works

Every bitcoin transaction goes through a process. You should remember that there are 3 parts of a bitcoin transaction: Input, Output, and the Amount. Let us take a look at them one by one:

✓ Input

Let us say that person A wants to send 2 bitcoins to person B. Before person A can send B 2 bitcoins, it is only logical that person A must first have 2 bitcoins in his wallet. This is what is referred to as the *input*. Simply put, it refers to the bitcoins in the sender's wallet, the amount of which should be greater than or at least equal to the amount that he wants to send to another.

✓ Output

The output refers to the receiver. In our example, it is person B. More specifically, it refers to the *wallet address* of person B. Take note that in a bitcoin transaction, you do not send the bitcoin directly to the name of the receiver. In a blockchain, the transfer of bitcoins is made between wallet addresses. Hence, if you are the sender, then you should first ask for the bitcoin wallet address of the receiver. It is to this wallet address where you will send bitcoins.

✓ Amount

Obviously, this refers to the amount that is involved in a transaction. In this case, the amount is 2 bitcoins.

What about mining?

Mining refers to the process of verifying, confirming, and adding blocks or records to the blockchain. In a bitcoin transaction, once miners confirm a transaction, it can no longer be canceled, withdrawn, or modified. As you can see, mining is an important part of the blockchain ecosystem. Without mining, no new block or record can be added to the blockchain. Hence, in a bitcoin blockchain, you can rest assured that there is always a demand for miners.

CHAPTER 4:
WHERE TO KEEP YOUR BITCOIN

Now, let us move on to the more practical side: Do you keep or store your bitcoins? Remember that there are two kinds of bitcoin wallets: the hot and cold wallet. Now, these two main categories of bitcoin wallets are further classified into several specific types. You need to understand their differences so that you will know which wallet type will best suit your needs. Let us look at them one by one:

- *Online Wallet*

An online wallet is the most common type of bitcoin wallet. It is also known as a *web wallet*. This is the most commonly used type of bitcoin wallet as it is very easy and convenient to use. Good examples of an online wallet are Coinbase and GreenAddress. This is the type of wallet that you can easily access and manage simply by going online and logging in to your wallet through the site provided by your wallet provider. However, take note that this is a hot wallet, so you cannot expect for it to be a secured as a cold wallet. The good news is that many of the reputable hot wallets have already updated their security features. But, if security is your main concern, then a cold wallet is still the best choice.

- *Mobile Wallet*

A mobile wallet is another type of hot wallet. It is also an online wallet; but this time, you should download the wallet application on your mobile phone. Normally, you can download the application for free at the Apple and/or GooglePlay store. Many people use their phones to access the Internet, so having a mobile version of your wallet can be really handy at times. Do not worry; many web wallets like GreenAddress and Coinbase also have a mobile version of their bitcoin wallet.

• *Desktop Wallet*

A desktop wallet is a type of cold wallet. When you use a desktop wallet, you will store your public and private keys on a computer, which may also be a laptop computer. Before you use any computer as a desktop wallet, you should first reformat your computer or at least ensure that it is free from any malware and virus. Also, once you start using a computer as a cold wallet, you should no longer connect it to the Internet. This is what makes a cold wallet more secure than a hot wallet. Once something is exposed to the Internet, then it gets exposed to online hazards like hackers, attackers, and viruses. Since cold wallets are held offline, they are free from such risks. This is what makes a desktop wallet and other cold wallets very secured.

• *Hardware Wallet*

A hardware wallet functions just like a desktop wallet. But, instead of storing your public and private keys in a computer, you get to store them in a hardware. Although you can use an ordinary USB for this purpose, such is not advisable since an ordinary USB does not have enough protective features and can get easily get corrupted. Different kinds of hardware wallets are sold in the market specially made for this purpose, such as the Ledger Nano. However, they can get expensive. The good news is that to date, there has been no report or issue of any hardware wallet getting hacked or compromised. Hence, this is definitely one of the best bitcoin wallets that you can use in terms of having a very high level of security.

• Paper Wallet

A paper wallet is another famous type of cold wallet. When you use a paper wallet, you get to store your private and public keys on a paper. You can print them on paper. Ideally, you should keep several copies. Needless to say, you should store them in a safe place where they will not be stolen. Take note that although cold wallets offer high security, this is only as far as online hazards are concerned. They still cannot protect you from thieves or from losing or breaking your cold wallet.

Which wallet type should you use?

When choosing the right wallet for you, you need to strike a balance between security and convenience. For convenience, then any of the hot wallets would be a good choice. If you want to focus more on security, then you should use a cold wallet.

When choosing a wallet, you should think about how you intend to use your bitcoins. If you know that you will most likely transact with bitcoins on a regular basis, then you should use a hot wallet. However, if you just want to make a long-term investment where you just want to keep your bitcoins for a period of time, then using a cold wallet would be a better choice.

You are also free to use several wallet types at the same time. Hence, you can have a cold wallet and a hot wallet at the same time. You can use a hot wallet for short-term investments and for your day-to-day transactions, and then you can use a cold wallet at the same time for your long-term investment in bitcoin. There are also professional bitcoin investors who use multiple hot and cold wallets at the same time. You may find this necessary once you have a high number of bitcoins. After all, it is not advisable to keep all your bitcoins in a single wallet despite how secured you believe it to be. As they say, "Do not put all your eggs in one basket." The same is true when it comes to storing and keeping your bitcoins.

CHAPTER 5:
BUYING BITCOIN

How do you buy bitcoins? Buying bitcoins is easy. In fact, there are hot wallets like Coinbase and coins.ph will allow you to purchase bitcoins directly from the wallet itself. Now, if this is not possible, then you can sign up for a trading account with a cryptocurrency trading broker. There are brokers like eToro that will allow you to deposit fiat money and buy bitcoins on the trading platform itself. You may also want to use *localbitcoins*. It is like a marketplace where people buy and sell bitcoins. However, you need to be cautious when you use such kind of cryptocurrency marketplace as there are many scammers out there. Another popular option is to buy bitcoins using PayPal by through Virwox. However, take note that this is not a suggested approach as the cost can get very expensive. Hence, there are only two suggested ways to buy bitcoins: Through your bitcoin wallet and a trustworthy cryptocurrency trading broker.

Buy price vs. Sell price

Before you purchase bitcoins, you first need to understand that there is a difference between the buy price and the sell price. The buy price is always higher than the sell price. This difference in price is how a broker or seller makes a profit. This also means that right after you buy bitcoins, you cannot just sell them immediately after their price fluctuates a little higher as you will most probably end up with a loss since the sell price will be lower than the price at which you bought your bitcoins. Be sure to keep this in mind both when selling and buying bitcoins.

Check the market price

Before you buy and sell bitcoins, be sure to check its current price in the market. Do not forget that the price of Bitcoin fluctuates rapidly. This is to ensure that you are buying/selling your bitcoins at a fair price. A good way to do this is to visit the site of well-known cryptocurrency traders like Bitfinex, Binance, and Bittrex. You can also check well-established websites that share information about the cryptocurrency market, such as *coinmarketcap* and *coingecko*.

Timing

Do not just buy bitcoins right away. Before you make a purchase, you should first study the cryptocurrency market. Do not forget that bitcoin has a high volatility and that its price continuously changes. You definitely would not want to buy bitcoin when its price is falling down. Therefore, it is important that you study the market and use proper timing. Take note that the price of bitcoin rises and falls; hence, you may have to enter (buy) and leave (sell) the market every now and then, depending on the circumstances. By taking the effort to study the market, you will be able to save yourself some money and even lower your expenses and losses. Keep in mind that you do not just enter the market at any time you want. You need to be objective about it, and only buy bitcoins if you think that now is the moment to make a profitable investment. It is not uncommon for professional investors to wait for a day or even a week before they purchase bitcoins, even though they are eager to invest. Once again, proper timing is important when buying, as well as when selling bitcoins.

When selling bitcoins, you would want to sell them when their price is about to fall. However, this may also depend on your strategy. If you are making a long-term investment, then you should expect to face various price fluctuations in the market, and this includes facing some price decreases. Do not worry; in a long-term investment, the only important thing is to be at a profit once you close your position (when you sell your bitcoins). Hence, even if the price falls by 30% after two weeks, it would not matter if you can profit, say, by 100% the following week or so. Of course, you would not be investing blindly. To turn the odds in your favor and significantly increase your chances of making a profit, you will have to use effective strategies (as discussed later in this book).

CHAPTER 6:
USING BITCOIN

Using bitcoin is very easy and convenient. As we have already discussed, many merchants accept payments in bitcoin. Today, there are also many people around the world who use bitcoins for remittance or for sending funds to people located in another country. Since the use of bitcoin effectively cuts away the middleman like banks, it is a good way to minimize your cost. Now let us discuss what you need to do when you use bitcoins:

✓ **Sending bitcoins**

If you are the one who will send bitcoins, then all you need to do is ask for the bitcoin wallet address of the person to whom you intend to send bitcoins. A bitcoin wallet address looks like a long string of random letters and numbers. Be sure to copy and paste it correctly. Do not forget that once a transaction is confirmed, there is no way that you can cancel, amend, withdraw it. Therefore, be very careful when sending bitcoins. Be sure that you send it to the correct bitcoin wallet address. To send bitcoins, just access your wallet, key in the amount that you want to send, and then paste the wallet address of the recipient, and just click *send*. This entire process can be completed in less than a minute. As you can see, it is very simple. The recipient will soon be notified in his wallet that there is a pending receivable. Once the transaction has passed through several confirmations, then he will be able to finally receive the bitcoins that you send to his account. This normally takes just a few minutes from the time of sending the bitcoins.

✓ **Receiving bitcoins**

If you are the recipient, then you simply have to give your bitcoin wallet address to the sender. Again, to avoid committing mistakes, you should simply copy and paste your wallet address when sharing it with the sender.

✓ Storing bitcoins

We have already discussed the different ways to store your bitcoins. Make sure to keep your bitcoin wallet safe and secured. There are certain strongly suggested practices that you should observe, such as using a strong password and allowing the two-factor authentication. Keep in mind that your bitcoin wallet password is your main line of defense against a hacker or anyone who would want to access your account without your consent. To have a strong password, you should combine both upper and lower case letter. You should also use numbers and symbols in your password. Last but not least, avoid simply using the minimum required a number of characters. Instead, use a long password of at least 15 characters long. Needless to say, do not use a password that other people can easily guess. The two-factor authenticator is another line of defense that your account has. When you enable it, a code will be sent to your phone when anyone tries to access your account. Normally, you will have to enter this code after entering your password. The code changes within a few seconds, so it is very hard to predict correctly. You may have to download Google Authenticator app to be able to view the code. Do not worry; you can easily download this application for free from the GooglePlay or Apple store. If you are using a cold wallet, be sure to keep it in a safe place where it will not be broken or stolen.

CHAPTER 7:
INVESTING IN BITCOIN

Investing in bitcoin follows the usual trader's maxim: Buy low, sell high. However, this is easier said than done. To be able to invest successfully in bitcoin, you need to use effective strategies. Here are some notable strategies that you should learn and practice:

» *Fundamental Analysis*

Fundamental analysis is probably the most important strategy that you should learn. It is also referred as the lifeblood of investment. When you use fundamental analysis, you should focus on the *basics* or the fundamentals that affect bitcoin. Therefore, you should follow on the news and be up-to-date with the latest developments. The key to using this strategy is to gather as much good-quality information as you can. As they say, "Knowledge is power." It is a basic rule in investing that the more that you know and understand a certain asset, the more likely that you will be able to predict its price movement in the market. The same applies when you invest in bitcoin or any other cryptocurrency. When you use fundamental analysis, you should research and analyze the news, economy, competition among the different cryptocurrencies, market acceptance, and the past and current trend of bitcoin, among many others. Indeed, fundamental analysis is probably the strategy that takes a lot of effort, but it is well worth it. In fact, if you are serious about being a professional bitcoin investor, then it is a must that you should learn and use fundamental analysis. After all, this strategy can easily be incorporated even when you are using another strategy.

It is also strongly suggested that you should join online groups and forums about bitcoin and other cryptocurrencies. This is a good way to gather more information. From time to time, you will definitely learn some interesting ideas and strategies from these groups and forums. Since you are investing in bitcoin, be sure to join and participate in the *bitcointalk* forum. If you do not want to participate, then at least read the posts and learn something from them. It is also worth mentioning that many cryptocurrency developers are active in such kind of forums and groups, and this can allow you to gain valuable information against the competitors of bitcoin. Indeed, if you are serious about making continuous profit y investing in bitcoin or any other cryptocurrency, fundamental analysis is the strategy that you should always use.

» *Technical Analysis*

Technical analysis is a favorite among many bitcoin investors. This strategy is good if you are more of a visual person who loves to study and analyze graphs. When you use technical analysis, you will be looking at graphs and charts that reflect the price movements of bitcoin. The idea behind this strategy is that all of the elements or factors that affect the price of bitcoin can be summed up and have their final effect on the price. Therefore, this goes to show that simply by dealing with the price movements of bitcoin, you also get to deal with the many factors and elements that affect bitcoin. Of course, the advantage of using this approach is that it is much simpler than fundamental analysis where you need to research, read, and analyze so many pieces of information and even involves computations (numbers).

When you use technical analysis, the key is to be able to identify and take advantage of patterns. Yes, patterns do exist. However, they also come and go. Therefore, do not expect to see a pattern every time that you look at a graph or chart. A common mistake is to force to see a pattern even when there is actually no pattern to be seen. So, if you do not see a pattern, accept that it is not there and do not force an investment.

Technical analysis is a good strategy for short-term investments, while fundamental analysis is usually the choice when it comes to making long-term investments. Still, technical analysis is something that you can easily incorporate regardless of the strategy that you are using. After all, you simply have to view a chart or graph. Your trading broker will usually provide you with such tools (charts) that you need. If you do not have a trading broker, then there are many websites online that you can visit to see the price movements of bitcoin (as well as other cryptocurrencies).

Although you can use and depend completely on technical analysis, real experts suggest that you should still make use of fundamental analysis. The problem with technical analysis is that it does not give you the reasons behind the price movements; hence, you can barely come up with an accurate prediction. The best way to use technical analysis is still to combine it with fundamental analysis. If you use both strategies together properly, you can significantly increase your chances of making a profitable investment.

» *Averaging Down*

This is a good strategy to use if you want to be able to make a high amount of profit from an investment. This will allow you to purchase bitcoin at a "bargain" price. Here is an example of how to use this strategy: Let us say, for example, that the current price of bitcoin is $10,000. The first step is to make a buy order at its current price. Hence, you should buy bitcoin at the said price of $10,000. Now, if the price of bitcoin increases, then you make a profit. However, if the price of bitcoin drops, say, down to $9,500, then you should make another buy order at the said lower amount of $9,500. Now, if the price decreases again, then you should make another buy order. The key is simply to keep buying it while its price in decreasing. Hence, you get to buy bitcoin at a "bargain."

Okay, so this may seem like as if you are merely purchasing a losing asset, but this is actually not the case. Just imagine how much you will profit once the price of bitcoin recovers and goes back to its original price (the price when you first used this strategy), or even higher. All the buy orders that you have made will experience a nice profit. This is also an excellent strategy to use to take advantage of the volatility of the market.

Although this strategy is very practical and effective, do not forget that it is still considered an aggressive strategy. Hence, you should be careful when you use this approach. The proper way of using this strategy is to research the market first. Only use this strategy if you think that the price of bitcoin will most likely increase in the near future. If after doing your research and analysis, there are good reasons to believe that the price of bitcoin will most likely increase, then that is the only time that you should use this strategy.

» *Quick Sell*

This strategy is a good way to earn small yet consistent profits. The key to using this strategy is not to be greedy and close your position before your risk of exposure gets high. Here is an example of how you should use this strategy. Let us assume that the price of bitcoin is worth $10,000. You make a buy order at its current price of $10,000. Now, if the price increases, say, up to $10,200, then you should make a sell order right away and enjoy the small return of profits. Again, this is a good way to take advantage of a volatile market.

Take note, however, that the sell price is much lower than the buy price. Be sure to check the prevailing rate and only sell your bitcoin if you can make a profit out of it.

When you use this strategy, you should first study the market, especially the current trend of bitcoin. The best time to apply this strategy is while the price of bitcoin is increasing. Enter the market when it is hot and leave it even when it still appears to be profitable. The longer that you hold your position, the greater is your exposure to risk. Do not forget that when you use this strategy, you should prioritize controlling your risk. Hence, be contented with a small profit, and then start over.

» *Wait It Out*

There are times when it can be difficult to invest in bitcoin. For example, as of the start of 2018, the price of bitcoin has been unstable. This does not mean that it is no longer a good investment. Rather, this only shows that it may not be a good time to invest in bitcoin at the moment. Again, this is part of the usual fluctuations that you can expect when you deal with any kind of cryptocurrency/ however, you can rest assured that this will soon change (which is part of the nature of the cryptocurrency market). So, do not be like the other investors who keep on investing even when the market is down. To minimize your risk and losses, you should only invest in bitcoin when it is profitable in the market. But, when you see that its price has constantly been falling for days and weeks, the best action would be to just be patient and keep watch. Soon, bitcoin will again be able to recover, and that is the time for you to invest as its price continues to increase.

Remember that no matter how eager you are to invest in bitcoin, you must be patient to wait for the right opportunity. The important thing is that you are ready to invest once that opportunity arises. Therefore, it is your job to continue to follow and study the market. Wait out the bad times and join the hot streaks. Pay close attention to the market.

» *Go with the Flow*

Bitcoin is not really that hard to predict. For example, when it was announced in the news that China would close down all its local cryptocurrency exchanges, bitcoin and altcoins experienced a drop in price. However, when the news featured that Russia started to legalize bitcoins, the price of bitcoin surged upwards. The same is true when bitcoin was featured on CNN showing just how profitable an investment it is. Again, when Singapore declared that it would not issue any restriction yet on bitcoin, the price of bitcoin also increased. As you can see, sometimes you just have to go with the flow, and you can easily make a profit. Bitcoin is not always hard to predict. In fact, most of the time, it is very easy to predict the direction that its price movement will take in the market.

When you go with the flow, it is still advised that you do your fundamental analysis to be sure that you are not being misdirected. Sometimes what you read online or see in the news can be deceiving, especially when there is a pump and dump scheme. What is a pump and dump scheme? This fraudulent scheme is nothing new. In fact, it has been used in the stock market for years and is now being used in the cryptocurrency market. In a pump and dump scheme, a group of people will promote a certain cryptocurrency using some form of promotional hype. Their objective is to draw as much as positive attention and interest as possible to drive the price of the promoted cryptocurrency higher. However, once its price increases as other investors continue to make investments thinking that it is a profitable cryptocurrency, the people behind the scheme will then sell the cryptocurrency being promoted at a nice profit. The final result is that those behind the scheme can make a good profit while the investors (victims of the scheme) will be holding a losing asset. Hence, for you not to fall victim to this scheme, be sure to do your own analysis of the market and do not just follow the flow without doing any research.

CHAPTER 8:
BITCOIN FOR BUSINESS

Businesses around the world also use Bitcoin. In fact, by using bitcoin in business, you can effectively cut down your cost as you would no longer need a middleman like banks and other financial sectors for sending and receiving money (cryptocurrency) to another. You have full control of everything. The process, as we have already discussed, is also very quick and simple. Indeed, many businesses use and accept bitcoins. Let us look at some of these known businesses that use bitcoin:

- *Microsoft*

Microsoft needs no introduction. This computer giant is known worldwide, and now it is also known for accepting payments in bitcoin when you buy from Windows or Xbox store.

- *Virgin Galactic*

This company engaged in space travel also accepts bitcoin. So, if you have lots of bitcoins in your possession, you can now buy your trip to space. The founder of Virgin Galactic openly admitted that he supports bitcoin cryptocurrency.

- *Wikipedia*

As you know, Wikipedia is a huge website where you can get tons of valuable information for free. Anyone who uses the Internet is familiar with Wikipedia. Well, although you can use Wikipedia for free, it is also known for accepting donations in bitcoin.

- *Tesla*

If you are interested in science and technology, perhaps you would also find it interesting to know that the company, Tesla, also uses and accepts payment in bitcoin. In fact, some of its inventions were funded using bitcoins.

• *Peach Airlines*

The Japanese airline known as Peach Airline also accepts payment in bitcoin. So, if you want to travel to another country and would love to pay for your airfare using bitcoins, you might want to buy your ticket from Peach Airlines

• *Steam*

Steam is a popular gaming platform with millions of registered and active users. You can now buy games and upgrades using bitcoins.

• *Overstock*

This company allows you to purchase big-ticket items. You can now buy products from Overstock using bitcoins. In fact, they have even partnered with a famous bitcoin wallet known as *Coinbase*.

Many other companies and businesses use and accept payments in bitcoin. Now, if you own a business, you can also take advantage of bitcoins by paying your employees in bitcoins. Just be sure to check if this is allowed in the laws of your country. Also, if your business normally involves sending and receiving funds, then you should really consider using bitcoins as it can effectively lower your expenses and will allow you to have complete control of the process. It is also good to use bitcoins if you are to send "money" to someone who is located in another country. The bitcoin system is open 24 hours a day every day; hence, you can easily send and receive bitcoins with just a few clicks of a mouse. If you are the recipient, then simply give your bitcoin wallet address to the sender, and just wait for him to send your bitcoins into your wallet.

CHAPTER 9:
BITCOIN MINING

Mining bitcoins is another investment that you might want to consider. As we have already discussed, there is always a demand for miners in the bitcoin blockchain; otherwise, there is no way for any record or transaction to be added to the chain and be completed. Now, there are different ways to mine bitcoins. Let us go over them one by one:

- *Computer mining*

This is the most basic way to mine for bitcoins. This is where you use your own computer for mining. You can do this by downloading GUIMiner and joining a mining pool. The suggested pool is the Slush's pool. However, this is only a good method to give you an experience of mining, but it is not a recommended method if you want to earn a decent amount of bitcoins. The reason is that a computer alone does not have sufficient hash power to mine a decent amount of bitcoins. You will most probably end up with more expenses on electricity than the actual amount of bitcoin that you could mine. Also, when you mine using your own computer, you will have to worry about overheating. Take note of this because this can break your computer's CPU. So, when it comes to earning a decent amount of bitcoins, this is not a recommended method. But, if you just want to experience how it feels like to mine bitcoins and earn a little, then this is a good start.

- *Hardware mining*

Since a computer alone is not enough to mine a decent amount of bitcoins due to its low mining power, you will have to use a mining hardware to increase your hash or mining power. There are websites online like Amazon and eBay where you can buy a mining hardware. It is noteworthy that even if you mine using a hardware, you still have to use your computer. Hence, you should still be careful about any overheating issues. You should follow a schedule that will allow your computer and mining hardware to cool down from time to time. In choosing a hardware, you should look at the mining power and also the electric consumption. It is not uncommon to find a strong mining hardware but then also consumes high electricity. You need to consider this to ensure that you will end up with a decent positive profit.

- *Could mining*

This seems to be the most famous method of mining bitcoins nowadays. With cloud mining, you no longer have to worry about any overheating issue. You do not even have to purchase any mining hardware. In fact, you do not even have to mine anything at all. Hence, you do not even have to use your computer. Instead, all that you need to do is to wait for the cloud mining company to send you bitcoins. You will usually receive your bitcoins every week or as soon as you meet the minimum threshold. Okay, this may sound too good to be true, so what is the catch? Of course, there is also a catch. After all, you cannot expect for any business to send you bitcoins every week just out of kindness. The catch is that you will first have to invest. This means that you must first pay a cloud mining company. Now, you have to be careful about this because there are many scammers online who simply want to rip you off of your money. Therefore, before you invest in any cloud mining company, you need to do your research, check the latest reviews given to the mining company, and learn as much as you can about the said company.

A usual offer may look something like this: Invest (or pay) 1 bitcoin and earn up to 0.035 bitcoins every week. Okay, so far this seems very ideal. You just have to make some simple computation, and you would already know when you can recover your investment, and then you can earn positive profits after that. However, this is not always the case. The problem is that the offer only shows the *expected* return and not the actual return of profits. This means that using the given example, you may receive less than 0.035 every week. Before you make any form of deposit or investment, you need to be sure that the terms and agreements of the contract are clear to you. In case of doubts, do not hesitate the customer support team, and they would be happy to assist you. Also, pay attention to the expiration date. There are cloud mining companies that only render the contract valid for a year — and so this means that you should be able to recover your investment and then earn profits within the same time period. Other cloud mining companies honor a lifetime validity of contract. Again, the best way to be sure about this is to read the contract and talk with the customer support team of the cloud mining company for clarifications.

CHAPTER 10:
SECURITY OF BITCOIN

So, is it safe and secure to use bitcoin? The answer is *yes*. Otherwise, companies would no longer be using it in business. Although there were reports in the past that certain bitcoin wallets had been hacked, it is worth noting that the security of both hot and cold wallets has already improved significantly. In fact, many professional investors these days only use a hot wallet or the trading account provided by their cryptocurrency trading broker. The point here is that in terms of security, you can rest assured that bitcoin has a high level of security. Also, do not forget the 51% attack concept. Today, bitcoin is well distributed over a very vast network of computers, so just imagine how much hash rate power an attacker needs to have to penetrate the bitcoin blockchain successfully.

As an investor, you no longer need to worry whether or not bitcoin is secure because it is. Your main concern is how to ensure the security of your bitcoin wallet. As we have already discussed, you may want to use a cold wallet for this purpose. If you are using a hot wallet, be sure to enhance the security of your wallet by using a strong password and also activate the two-factor authentication or any other security features that your wallet provider may offer.

Bitcoin is also a continuously evolving technology, so you can expect for its security features to get even stronger and more secure over time. The good news is that as far as security is concerned, it can now be said that bitcoin is very secure. Hence, so many individuals and known businesses are using it, and many are still eager to learn about it so that they can also take advantage of the benefits of using bitcoin. In fact, there are those who believe that bitcoin is even more secure than traditional banks. As bitcoin continues to grow and dominate the cryptocurrency market, you can expect for more developments and improvements to happen over time.

CONCLUSION

Thanks for making it through to the end of this book. We hope it was informative and able to provide you with all of the tools you need to achieve your goals whatever they may be.

The next step is to apply everything that you have learned and start earning serious profits. Unfortunately, many people still think that bitcoin is a bubble that is about to burst. Well, it is up to you whether or not you want to believe this heresy. However, as far as the truth is concerned, those who believe that bitcoin is just a bubble failed to make any profit from it, while those who have taken the risk and believe in bitcoin as a profitable investment can earn a high amount of profits, even their way to complete financial freedom.

Finally, if you found this book useful in anyway, a review on Amazon is always appreciated!

ETHEREUM

The Ultimate Guide to the World of Ethereum

By Sam Sutton

~~~

© Copyright 2018 By Sam Sutton
All Rights Reserved

The transmission, duplication or reproduction of any of the following work including specific information will be considered an illegal act irrespective of if it is done electronically or in print. This extends to creating a secondary or tertiary copy of the work or a recorded copy and is only allowed with express written consent from the Publisher. All additional right reserved.

The information in the following pages is broadly considered to be a truthful and accurate account of facts and as such any inattention, use or misuse of the information in question by the reader will render any resulting actions solely under their purview. There are no scenarios in which the publisher or the original author of this work can be in any fashion deemed liable for any hardship or damages that may befall them after undertaking information described herein. This book should not be taken as financial or investment advice, and the author does not take any responsibility for inaccuracies, omissions, or errors which may be found therein.

Additionally, the information in the following pages is intended only for informational purposes and should thus be thought of as universal. As befitting its nature, it is presented without assurance regarding its prolonged validity or interim quality. Trademarks that are mentioned are done without written consent and can in no way be considered an endorsement from the trademark holder.

The contents of this book are intended to convey general information only. You should not treat any information herein as a call to make any particular decision regarding cryptocurrency usage, legal matters, investments, taxes, cryptocurrency mining, exchange usage, wallet usage, etc. It is strongly suggested that you seek advice from your own financial, investment, tax, or legal adviser. This book should not be taken as financial or investment advice, and the author does not take any responsibility for inaccuracies, omissions, or errors. The author of this work is not responsible for any loss, damage, or inconvenience caused as a result of reliance on information as published on, or linked to, this book.

The author of this book has taken careful measures to share vital information about the subject. May its readers acquire the right knowledge, wisdom, inspiration, and succeed.

TABLE OF CONTENTS

Introduction 53

Chapter 1: What is Ethereum? 55

Chapter 2: The Technology Behind Ethereum 59

Chapter 3: What is Ethereum Mining? 61

Chapter 4: Uses of Ethereum 65

Chapter 5: What is Ether? 69

Chapter 6: Financial History of Ether 71

Chapter 7: How to Buy, Sell, and Store Ether 73

Chapter 8: The Mining Process of Ether 83

Chapter 9: Should I Invest in Ether? 85

Chapter 10: The Future of Ethereum 87

INTRODUCTION

Congratulations on downloading this book and thank you for doing so.

Countless of people want to learn how to invest in cryptocurrencies, especially in Ethereum. The reason is that such investment has a very high-profit potential. Indeed, there are many success stories of people around the world who have made a fortune simply by investing in cryptocurrencies. Today, Ethereum is considered by many experts as one of the most lucrative investments in the market. In fact, there are those who believe that Ethereum will finally surpass Bitcoin in the near future.

The following chapters will teach you the ins and outs of Ethereum, as well as how you can make a profitable investment and enjoy the flow of profits.

Chapter 1 talks about what Ethereum is all about. This will give you a good foundation and understanding of Ethereum.

Chapter 2 discusses the technology behind Ethereum. Understand the Ethereum blockchain, so that you will know how Ethereum works.

Chapter 3 talks about the different ways to mine ether. Mining is another option that you have if you want to invest in Ethereum.

Chapter 4 discusses the various uses of Ethereum. Since Ethereum promotes the use of smart contracts and distributed applications, it has limitless uses and possibilities.

Chapter 5 talks about ether, which is the token and what powers the whole Ethereum blockchain.

Chapter 6 shows the financial history of ether from a very low and negligible value up to its current value that is worth more than a thousand dollars.

Chapter 7 discusses how to buy, sell, and store ether. This is also the chapter that will teach you how to make money by investing in ether.

Chapter 8 explains the mining process of ether.

Chapter 9 talks about why you should invest in ether. Some so many people are eager to invest in ether. Find out why investing in this cryptocurrency is such a highly lucrative investment.

Chapter 10 discusses the future of Ethereum. Learn why investing in Ethereum today might just be the best investment that you can ever make.

May this book be your guiding light to success and financial freedom.

There are plenty of books on this subject on the market, thanks again for choosing this one! Every effort was made to ensure it is full of as much useful information as possible. Please enjoy!

CHAPTER 1:
WHAT IS ETHEREUM?

Ethereum is an open and decentralized blockchain platform that allows its users to run decentralized applications on blockchain technology. Similar to Bitcoin, no one owns or manipulates the Ethereum protocol. It is considered as an open-source project that allows the use of smart contracts.

Ethereum was developed and proposed by Vitalik Buterin back in 2013. It received its funding from a crowdsale in 2014. A year after or in 2015, Ethereum was finally launched in the market.

Ethereum has long been considered as the second most successful cryptocurrency in the world next to Bitcoin. As of January 14, 2008, the price of 1 ether (Ethereum token) is around USD 1,430.

What is a *Cryptocurrency*?

Before we continue to discuss the details behind this *cryptocurrency*, you should first understand what a cryptocurrency is. A cryptocurrency is a type of digital asset. It is held and stored electronically (online). Take note that it does not have a physical existence. A cryptocurrency differs from fiat money in the sense that fiat money is the recognized and official currency of a state like the US dollar. A cryptocurrency is also not considered to be legal tender. In law, legal tender refers to that which the debtor can compel his creditor to accept payment. Of course, the exception to this rule is if it is stipulated in the contract that payment may be made in cryptocurrency.

Cryptocurrency is secured using *cryptography*. This refers to the practice of turning information into codes. Cryptography was extensively used during the Second World War since it was important to ensure that the security of information communicated in the army was protected against enemy spies. This is how trustworthy and reliable cryptography is.

Today, there are more and more individuals and merchants who accept payments in cryptocurrencies, such as Microsoft, Overstock, Steem, Fiverr, Virgin Galactic, and many others.

Who is Vitalik Buterin?

Unlike the founder of Bitcoin whose identity remains anonymous, the co-founder of Ethereum is well known to the public. Vitalik Buterin is said to be the mind behind the Ethereum cryptocurrency. He is a young Russian-Canadian computer programmer born in 1994. He is also a co-founder of the famous, Bitcoin Magazine. It was his father who introduced to him the world of cryptocurrency. His father taught him about bitcoin when Vitalik was only 17 years old. Since then Vitalik placed his focus on learning more about the technicalities and codings behind cryptocurrencies, which soon led him to come up with the white paper for Ethereum.

What are Smart Contracts?

Smart contracts are a form of computer protocol that can execute contracts provided certain conditions are met. As such, they effectively enforce the execution of contracts and ensure that they are executed according to the prescribed conditions. Smart contracts cannot yet handle complicated tasks, but you can always use many smart contracts to handle and fully execute such tasks.

The term *smart contracts* is nothing new. It was first coined back in 1996 by Nick Szabo. The concept was developed over the course of several years. Back then, Nick Szabo defined smart contracts as follows: New institutions, and new ways to formalize the relationships that make up these institutions, are now made possible by the digital revolution. I call these new contracts "smart," because they are far more functional than their inanimate paper-based ancestors. No use of artificial intelligence is implied. A smart contract is a set of promises, specified in digital form, including protocols within which the parties perform on these promises.

Ethereum as an Altcoin

Ethereum is considered as an *altcoin*. An altcoin is simply a term that is short for *alternative coin*. In the cryptocurrency market, all cryptocurrencies that are not a bitcoin are considered as altcoins. To date, there are more than 1,000 altcoins that have already been developed and launched in the market, and the number keeps on increasing. Ethereum is one of these altcoins. However, unlike the majority of altcoins in the market, Ethereum, is one of the most successful, popular, and profitable cryptocurrencies in the market today. In fact, many experts claim that Ethereum will soon be able to take Bitcoin's place as the number one cryptocurrency in the world.

It is worth noting that there is nothing wrong with being considered as an altcoin. In fact, many investors these days are more interested in altcoins than in bitcoin. Altcoins like Ethereum usually have a big room for development; hence, their profit potential is also high.

Crypto Kitties

When you read about Ethereum, you will most likely encounter the term *Crypto Kitties*. Okay, these Crypto Kitties are a new invention launched in the latter part of 2017. They are like the classic toy, Tamagotchi, where you take care of a virtual pet. In this case, you will take care of a virtual cat that runs on the Ethereum Blockchain. This is an Ethereum-based game where you can take care of and breed a virtual cat. So, what makes this significant? Well, some people buy and sell these virtual cats. Just to give you an idea of how significant this matter is: People all over the world have already spent more than 6.5 million dollars on these crypto kitties. The thing is that you can sell them also at a profit. Based on the record, the *genesis cat*, which is said to be the most expensive crypto kitty was sold for $115,000.

If you look closely, the virtual cats themselves are just part of what makes this whole Crypto Kitty thing of any significance. The important thing to note is the possibility that it creates in the world of Ethereum and cryptocurrencies. This is just the beginning. In fact, this only signifies the possible uses and extent of Ethereum's blockchain technology. Imagine being able to sell and transact other things like stocks and gold, etc. using Ethereum in the near future. Well, it is worth mentioning that owning a crypto kitty can also be fun. It is like owning a Tamagotchi. However, this time, you can sell it at a high profit.

CHAPTER 2:
THE TECHNOLOGY BEHIND ETHEREUM

Ethereum is based on blockchain technology. Blockchain technology is a kind of decentralized, public, and distributed ledger that records all transactions. It also has a high security. It is composed or records called *blocks*. Every new block that is added to the chain is connected to a previous block. This makes all the blocks interconnected with one another. The blockchain technology, or simply *blockchain*, is spread over a vast network of computers. Once a block is added to the chain, there is no way for it to be changed, modified, or altered, without changing or affecting other blocks. For any amendment to take place, there has to be consent from at least 51% of the users in the network. This is known as the *51% concept*. According to this concept, for any attack against the blockchain to be successful, it must possess at least 51% of the hash rate of the entire blockchain network. Since the network is spread over many computers/users, this is virtually impossible. Hence, blockchain has a high level of security. Take note that the 51% concept refers to the success of an attack and not to the possibility of being attacked.

It is worth noting that the Ethereum blockchain is the platform. It is powered by its token known as *ether*. The Ethereum blockchain is not just any other kind of blockchain. It also promotes the use of smart contracts and distributed applications. It is the presence of distributed applications that allows it to interact with the blockchain using smart contracts. The smart contracts run on every node of the Ethereum blockchain, which makes the application to be distributed.

There is also what is called as the *Ethereum Virtual Machine* or simply referred to as EVM. The EVM is the environment that runs and processes smart contracts. All the nodes in the Ethereum network that has a smart contract are run by EVM. It allows transactions to be made and actions to be automatically executed on the Ethereum blockchain.

In an Ethereum transaction, there is also what is called as gas. This term simply refers to the internal pricing for processing a transaction or contract on the Ethereum blockchain. Keep in mind that the Ethereum blockchain is powered by *ether*. The gas simply refers to the amount of ether that is needed to process and complete a transaction. It is often simply referred to as a transaction fee.

CHAPTER 3:
WHAT IS ETHEREUM MINING?

Before learning how to mine Ethereum tokens (ETH), you should first understand the importance of mining. In a blockchain, before any new block or record is added, the transaction first needs to be verified and confirmed before it can be added to the blockchain. This process of verification is important as you can no longer remove or alter a block once it is added to the chain without affecting all the other blocks. Hence, there is always a demand for miners. Also, take note that you are not mining for Ethereum literally. Remember that Ethereum is the platform; what you are mining for is Ethereum's token known as *ether (ETH)*. Let us examine them one by one:

- **CPU mining**

This is also referred to as computer mining. This is where you mine ether simply by using your computer's CPU. This is easy to do and is a recommended mining method for beginners who simply want to experience what it means to actually mine cryptocurrencies like Ethereum. There are several ways of doing this. A simple way is to download the GUI miner known as MinerGate. Simply go to www.minergate.com and follow the instructions for creating an account. Do not worry; it is as simple as creating a new email or Facebook account. You can complete the whole process within a few minutes. You can then use the software to mine ether.

The problem with CPU mining is that you will most probably end up with more electricity expense than the amount of ether that you will earn. This is because CPU mining alone does not have enough hash power to mine a decent amount of cryptocurrency. Another issue that you may encounter is overheating. When you mine using your computer, you should follow a schedule; otherwise, your CPU might overheat and could even be broken.

If you are serious about making a profit by mining cryptocurrency like ether, then you should use a hardware. CPU mining is good only if you starting out and just want to experience mining cryptocurrency, but you cannot expect to make any decent profit from it. This leads us to the next method of mining known as *hardware mining*.

- **Hardware mining**

Since one's computer alone does not generate enough mining power to earn a decent amount of cryptocurrency, you need to use a hardware to allow you to increase your mining power. Take note that when you use a hardware, you still have to use your computer, so you should still be careful with any overheating issues. A good way to prevent this is by following a schedule. Be sure to give your CPU and mining hardware enough time to cool down.

When you do hardware mining for Ethereum, you will have to use a specialized hardware called as *Graphics Processing Unit* (GPU). Before, the developers of Ethereum thought that ether can effectively be mined using ordinary CPUs; but then they later discovered that using GPUs is way better and more profitable. There are many GPUs in the market. When choosing which GPU to use, you need to strike a balance between the high hash rate power (mining power) and electric consumption. You can find many GPUs on sale on eBay and Amazon. Before you purchase any mining hardware, be sure to do your research and check the latest reviews. There are three main drawbacks of using a mining hardware: First, a high-quality mining hardware can be costly. Second, you have to worry about your electric expenses since you will be mining for hours on a regular basis; and third, you will still have to deal with overheating issues.

- **Cloud mining**

Cloud mining is one of the most popular ways to mine ether and other cryptocurrencies these days. With cloud mining, you would not have to worry about buying any hardware or downloading a software. In fact, you do not even have to bother about any overheating issue as you do not even have to use your computer to mine. Instead, a mining company will do all the work for you. All that you need to do is to wait for the mining company to send you ether, which is usually on a weekly basis or as soon as you reach the minimum payout threshold.

Okay, that sounds great. Now, what is the catch? Of course, no mining company would send you cryptocurrency just for nothing. The catch is that you will have to make an investment. Normally, you may see something like this: Invest or pay 1 ether and receive 0.023 ether every week. Although this may seem like an ideal deal, especially in the long run, it is not always that desirable. The problem here is that what the cloud mining company reveals to you is only the *expected* return and not the *actual* return that you will get. Therefore, in our given example, it is possible that you may only receive 0.01 ether in a week, or even lower. It is also common for cloud mining companies to impose an expiration of the contract, while others may allow a lifetime contract. As a rule of thumb, before you invest in any cloud mining company, make sure that you read the latest reviews and read the terms and conditions of the contract carefully. If there is any part in the contract that is not clear to you, do not hesitate to contact the customer support team.

CHAPTER 4:
USES OF ETHEREUM

Ethereum is a platform that allows the use of smart contracts and distributed applications on its blockchain. This makes it highly versatile and usable for many purposes. Of course, with its token known as *ether*, it can also function as any other cryptocurrency that works as a substitute for money. But, Ethereum has taken this a step further. With the use of smart contracts and distributed applications, the Ethereum platform can do lots of things, such as create other platforms, games, messengers, function as the base support of other altcoins, and many others.

As we have already discussed, Ethereum is composed of a vast computer network. There are thousands of computers connected to it. This is what makes it a decentralized network. This means that the computers that form the Ethereum network cannot be controlled, shut down, or manipulated by any entity, group, or individual. This, together with the use of smart contracts and distributed applications, opens the door to various uses and applications of Ethereum. Here are some examples:

- **Transactions**

Ethereum can be used for the exchange of things of value. You can be sure that it will be risk-free. With the use of smart contracts, a transaction will only be executed and completed once certain conditions are met. This can also lower your cost involved in a transaction as it effectively removes any third-party service in a transaction. Ethereum has an IFTTT logic in its system. This refers to the "IF This Then That" logic. Once certain conditions are met, then execution of the contract can be made. Since it effectively removes the middleman in a transaction, then you can save on cost, especially in the long run.

- **Security against hackers**

Ethereum can be used to protect you from hackers and other online attacks. As you already know by now, the Ethereum blockchain has a high security. It is virtually impossible to break into it. Hence, you can rest assured that your any sensitive data can remain protected.

- **Health records**

Another use of the Ethereum blockchain is the recording and storage of hospital records. This can be used, especially when developing vaccines or in the process of treatment. For example, you can easily have a check-up in Canada and be treated in the U.S. easily since you have all your records stored in the Ethereum blockchain. This can also be used by doctors and hospitals in sharing valuable information with one another.

- **High-technology innovations**

Ethereum can be used in the creation and development of high-technology innovations, such as self-driving cars and even self-piloted aircrafts. The possibilities that can be harnessed by the Ethereum platform are definitely way beyond how an ordinary cryptocurrency like bitcoin works. After all, Ethereum is far more than a cryptocurrency that functions as a medium of exchange. Instead, it encourages and drives the development of technology, which makes it open to limitless possibilities.

- **Effective storage of data**

Regardless what kind of data or information that you want to store, you can rest for sure that it will be protected and secured when you use Ethereum. You no longer have to depend on a few servers and worry that they might get hacked or broken. With Ethereum, you can store data in thousands of computer networks spread across the world. With Ethereum, you can encrypt and send data to millions of servers very quickly.

- **Casino gambling**

There are many cryptocurrency gambling sites today. You no longer have to drive just to visit a casino. You can gamble online in the comfort of your home using ether. There are also many live casinos that will allow you to play casino games with a real and professional dealer.

- **Profitable investment**

It is not a secret that majority of those who own ethers use them as a form of investment. In fact, many people these days are so eager to learn about cryptocurrencies with a hope that they can make money out of the cryptocurrency market. The good news is that this is possible. In fact, there are already many people around the globe who have earned millions of dollars, and some have even attained financial freedom by investing in cryptocurrencies like Ethereum. Investing in Ethereum can be a highly lucrative investment. Just in 2017, the price of Ethereum in the market has increased by around 13,000%, and that translates to 13,000% profit had you made an investment in the same year. Take note that this does not include its many other price increases in the previous years. Here is the good news: If you take a closer look at the past and future trend of Ethereum, it is not hard to recognize that it still remains to be a highly lucrative investment today. In fact, many experts agree that the price of Ethereum will most probably increase significantly this 2018 to the point that it might be able to overtake Bitcoin and soon be the number one cryptocurrency in the market.

Additional Notes

There are, of course, many other uses and applications of Ethereum. Its platform is like a rich soil on which you can grow many wonderful trees. This will depend on how you use it, especially with respect to the use of smart contracts and distributed applications on the Ethereum blockchain. It should also be noted that although Ethereum has already gained a worldwide popularity and positive reputation, it is nonetheless still a young technology. This means that it still has a big room for improvement and growth. Now, this is actually a good thing, especially if the developers behind this cryptocurrency truly excel in what they are doing.

CHAPTER 5:
WHAT IS ETHER?

Ether is important to Ethereum as it serves as the fuel for the entire network. It is also the payment that clients make to the machines for the execution of their requested operations. Simply put, ether keeps the entire Ethereum blockchain network working and functioning. Without ether, then the whole Ethereum blockchain system will just cease to work.

Creation of Ether

The whole supply of ether was decided back during its presale in 2014 from the donations that it received. The developers of Ethereum have revealed the figures on the Ethereum website. To the contributors of the presale, a total of 60 million ether were made. Twelve percent of this number was assigned as a development fund. To a miner of a block, 5 ethers are made. Last but not least, 2 to 3 ethers may be sent to another miner if he can find a solution but fails to have his block included.

Ether Supply

It should be noted that ether has a finite number. Just like any other cryptocurrency, it would lose its value if it ever had an infinite supply. As agreed upon on the presale, ether has a cap at 18,000,000 every year. This number represents 25% of the initial supply. However, take note that according to the latest update from its developers, Ethereum will take a new consensus algorithm, which will be called as Casper. This is expected to take place in the year 2018 or 2019. According to the developers, this will make the system more efficient and would also make it easier to mine ether. Hence, it is important for you to keep a close watch as to the latest updates and future updates, especially those updates that come directly from the developers of Ethereum.

Do You Need Ether?

Simply put, for as long as you want to use the Ethereum platform, then you need to have ether. Otherwise, there is no way that you can make use of this platform. If you are a developer who wants to build your application based on Ethereum blockchain, then you need ether. The same is true if you want to make use of the smart contracts on the Ethereum blockchain. It is also worth mentioning that if you simply want to make an investment in this profitable and continuously rising cryptocurrency, then you should buy and/or earn ether for yourself.

It is worth noting that as compared to the price of bitcoin, ether can still be considered cheap. If you honestly think that ether will be successful in the market, then experts suggest that you should start investing in it as soon as possible just before its price gets as expensive as, if not more expensive than bitcoin. After all, the only way that you can truly take advantage of Ethereum is if you possess ether since ether is the lifeblood of the Ethereum blockchain.

CHAPTER 6:
FINANCIAL HISTORY OF ETHER

Let us study the price history of ether over the years. In 2014, ether was introduced in the market. Of course, as can be expected of any other new altcoin, it did not have any significant value. It started out slow. In 2015, ether reached its $1 milestone and started to draw more attention from a few cryptocurrency investors and traders. It was unstable up to the end of 2015 with its price going and fluctuating below a dollar. However, in the latter part of January 2016, it started to cross the $1 milestone again and got even more established. In April 2016, it already crossed more than $10. It continued to grow slowly. Of course, it was also subject to the usual fluctuations in price that is inherent in the cryptocurrency market, but you could easily recognize that its price was slowly but constantly increasing. At the beginning of 2017, it experienced a loss that its price dropped down to $8. However, starting that period, the price of ether started to grow quickly. In April of the same year, its price reached $48. Within three months, its price rocketed to $283. Before the end of 2017, its price was close to $1,000. As of January 14, 2018, the price of 1 ether is around $1,430. Since it continues to draw more attention and interest in the market, many professional investors claim that its price will continue to grow. All known cryptocurrency exchanges now include ether in the list of its cryptocurrencies being traded. In fact, some experts agree that 2018 is most likely the year that ether will take the place of bitcoin as the number one cryptocurrency in the market.

This is the financial history of ether up to January 14, 2018. The good news is that when you read the current news on the cryptocurrency market, there are so many positive news pieces about ether and Ethereum in general. There are also many new altcoins that are based on the Ethereum platform. Needless to say, this also boosts the price of ether in the market. Although the future of ether remains unknown, there are good reasons to believe that this 2018 will most likely be the biggest hit and price leap that Ethereum will make. Considering relevant factors, including the current position of Ethereum in the market and how it is perceived as a cryptocurrency, there is more than 75% probability that this 2018 is the best moment to invest in Ethereum.

Of course, just like investing in any other cryptocurrency, it is important for you to do your research and have a closer look at the market. You should never underestimate the high volatility of the market. Therefore, even though circumstances show just how highly profitable investing in ether would most likely be this 2018, make sure that you do your own research and analysis of the market, and make your investment wisely.

Just like other cryptocurrencies, ether is also subject to the usual fluctuations in price in the market. This is normal and is considered as innate part of the cryptocurrency market. However, the important thing is to see its price behavior in a long-term perspective. It cannot be denied that Ethereum has been growing steadily and significantly these past weeks to the point that its growth appears to be unstoppable. Another good news is that the more that it grows, the more attention it draws to itself, and so the more investors are willing to make an investment in Ethereum. This, of course, will push its price even higher than it already is. Unlike other assets, cryptocurrencies like Ethereum work like social media in the sense that the more it establishes itself and broadens its network, the stronger and more profitable it becomes. Indeed, there is so much to expect from Ethereum, especially this 2018. Although this is still a mystery to be uncovered, many believe that Ethereum is going to dominate the market this 2018.

CHAPTER 7:
HOW TO BUY, SELL, AND STORE ETHER

This is probably the most interesting part of the book as this chapter will teach you how you can actually make a profit by buying and selling ether. Now, before you can start buying and selling ether for profit, you first need to have a place where you can store ether. This is referred to as an Ethereum/ether wallet. There are several kinds of wallets that you can use. For starters, there are two main kinds. They are the hot and cold wallets. A hot wallet is the kind of cryptocurrency wallet (also applies in other cryptocurrencies and not just for ether) that is stored and held completely online. There is also what is known as a cold wallet, also known as *cold storage*. This is the kind of wallet where you keep your public and private keys offline. So, how are they different from each other? Well, let us just say that a hot wallet is more convenient to use since all you need is an Internet connection to access and manage this kind of wallet. However, since a hot wallet is exposed to the hazards of the Internet, it is exposed to risks. It can be a target of hackers and even be attacked by viruses and malware. This is where a cold wallet comes into the picture. A cold wallet is not exposed to the Internet; therefore, it offers more security. However, it is not as convenient to use as a hot wallet. Now that you know the two main types of cryptocurrency wallets let us quickly go through their specific types. Hot and cold wallets are further divided into the following:

- **Web wallet**

This is a kind of hot wallet that is completely accessible and manageable online. Hence, it is also referred to as an *online wallet*. This is the most common type of wallet used by a majority of Ethereum and cryptocurrency users. If you are just starting out, it is strongly advised that you try opening an Ethereum web wallet. A good place, to begin with, is Coinbase since it will allow you to buy and sell ether directly from your Coinbase wallet.

- **Mobile wallet**

A mobile wallet is a hot wallet that you can download on your mobile phone. Most web wallets are also mobile wallets. Normally, you can download the wallet as an application for free from the GooglePlay and/or Apple store.

- **Desktop wallet**

A desktop wallet is kind of cold wallet. When you use a desktop wallet, you store your private and public keys on a computer. The computer does not necessarily have to be a desktop-type computer; hence, a laptop computer will work just fine. Just be sure that it is free from viruses and malware, and do not connect it to the Internet once you start using it as a cold wallet.

- **Hardware wallet**

A hardware wallet is another type of cold wallet. It also works just like a desktop wallet; however, this time you will store your public and private keys on a hardware, such as a USB or a hardware that is specially made for this purpose.

- **Paper wallet**

A paper wallet is a popular type of cold wallet. When you use this wallet, you will store your public and private keys on a paper. Normally, you will be asked to print some codes on a paper. It is also common to include a QR code that you can scan. Without the paper, you will not be able to access and/or move cryptocurrency from your account to another. Hence, the paper is required for any transaction to be made. Needless to say, you should keep it in a safe place. It is advised that you keep several copies just in case you might lose a copy.

- **Additional tip: Trading Broker Account as a Wallet**

Many investors and traders simply use the trading account provided by their broker as a wallet. After all, it is also a place where you can store ether and even other cryptocurrencies. However, if you simply want to invest in Ethereum for a long-term, then you may no longer need a trading broker as you can usually purchase and also sell ether directly from a wallet such as Coinbase. So, if you just want to deal with Ethereum alone, then you may skip the need of working with a trading broker; however, if you want to trade ether as well as other cryptocurrencies, then signing up for an account with a cryptocurrency trading broker like Bitfinex and binance is important. You may also want to have a trading account in cases where you cannot purchase ether or any other cryptocurrency directly from your wallet. There are traders like eToro that will allow you to buy ether in exchange for fiat money, while others will first require you to deposit bitcoins and have them exchanged for ether on the platform. This may vary from trader to trader, so be sure to learn and understand as much as you can about the trading broker. Be sure to read the terms and conditions.

Cryptocurrency Trading Broker

Here are some of the things that you should look at choosing a trading broker. Keep in mind that if you want to buy and sell ether and other cryptocurrencies, it is important that you work only with a trustworthy broker:

- **Latest reviews**

Of course, just like before you use any service or products that are offered online, the first step is always to check the latest reviews and see what other people say about it. The same applies when choosing a trading broker. Be sure to read the reviews and take note of the dates when the reviews were written.

- **Customer Support**

The broker has to have an active and professional customer support team. You will find this helpful, especially if you encounter some technical problems in the future. Normally, a broker will provide you with an email address where you can contact the support team. It may also provide an on-page live chat service or even a number that you may call for inquiries.

- **Withdrawal requirements**

It is usually fast and easy when making a deposit; however, problems may arise when making a withdrawal. It is common for trading brokers to request for certain documents to be submitted prior to processing a withdrawal request. They may require you to submit a copy of a valid ID and a proof of billing. Before you make any deposit, you should make sure that you have such documents available in your possession to avoid problems in the future. Feel free to contact the support team to be clear about this matter. You should also check how many days it will take your broker to complete a withdrawal request. Ideally, a broker should be able to send to you your requested withdrawal within 24 hours, provided that you have already submitted the required documents.

- **Trading platform**

Your broker is the one who will provide you with a platform for trading cryptocurrencies. Since you want to invest in ether, then the platform should make it easy for you to buy and sell ether at any time that you want. It should also provide you with free tools, such as price charts, to help you understand how ether is performing in the market. This is essential, especially if you are fond of using technical analysis.

- **Mobile feature**

These days, it is much easier to access the Internet through a mobile device. Not only should your broker provide you with a trading platform, but it should also allow you to buy and sell ether directly from your mobile phone. Do not worry; most, if not all, reliable trading brokers always have a mobile version of the trading platform.

Buying and Selling Ether Tips and Tricks

It is now time to discuss the best practices that you should observe when you buy and sell ether for profit. Pay close attention to these tips and tricks to increase your chances of success.

- **Buy low, sell high**

This is the most common advice given to traders. The same applies when you invest in ether: Buy low, sell high. Take note that this does not mean that you have to wait for the price of ether to drop down back to $2 for this will most likely not happen anymore. Buying low simply means buying it at a price that is lower when you get to sell it. Hence, although the price of a single ether these days is worth more than a thousand dollars, it is still "low" provided that you can sell it at a higher price. So, the important thing to note here is to identify if the price of ether will most likely increase. If yes, then you should make a buy order. Of course, for you to be able to predict the price movement of ether in the market, you cannot just rely on luck or mere guesswork. You need to research and analyze the market. When it comes to understanding how ether performs in the cryptocurrency market, you should learn two important strategies: fundamental analysis and technical analysis.

- **Fundamental Analysis**

Fundamental analysis is rightly called the lifeblood of investment for good reasons. This approach deals with the fundamentals which means that it deals directly with the basics. Predicting the price movement of ether or any other cryptocurrency mainly depends on how well you understand the basic factors or elements that have an influence over it price, such as the economy, the level of competition among the different cryptocurrencies in the market, the latest news, market acceptance, government regulations, and technological developments and breakthroughs, among others. When you use fundamental analysis, the key is to gather as much quality information as you can. As the saying goes, "Knowledge is power." The more knowledge that you have not only about ether but also about the whole cryptocurrency market itself, the more likely that you can "read" and predict the direction that ether will most likely take in the market. When you use this approach, it is important for you to pay attention to the news as it can strongly affect ether and other cryptocurrencies. For example, when a positive news piece about Ethereum was featured on Google and CNN, the price of Ether surged even further. If you are serious about making continuous profit, then fundamental analysis should be part of your day-to-day activity as a cryptocurrency investor.

- **Technical Analysis**

If there is fundamental analysis, then there is also technical analysis. Technical analysis is where you study the price movements (past and current trend) of a particular cryptocurrency as shown by graphs or charts. This is an excellent strategy if you are more of a visual person. Indeed, it is also much simpler than fundamental analysis which is why so many investors like this approach. The idea behind this strategy is that all of the factors that can affect a cryptocurrency (in this case, ether) have their final effect on the price. Therefore, by simply analyzing the price of ether, you also get to deal and analyze all the factors that have an influence on it. If you like taking advantage of patterns and trends, then this is the one for you. It is worth noting, however, that technical analysis alone may not always be enough. Many experts agree that to further increase the effectiveness of this strategy, you should combine it fundamental analysis, and that mastery of the two can increase your chances of making the right investment decision by more than 75%.

- **Research**

Research is definitely in the heart of every successful investment. This is a very important part of fundamental analysis. If you want to improve your chances of success significantly, then you should do your research. A common mistake is not doing continuous research. Keep in mind that ether has a high volatility, especially these days when it is constantly experiencing high surges in price. You need to be up-to-date with the latest news and developments. Another common mistake is not doing enough research. It is true that many investors do their research prior to making an investment; however, the problem is that many of them do not render sufficient research. Just because you have studied a particular graph for about three hours does not mean that you are already in the position to make a sound investment decision. You should know that professional and successful cryptocurrency investors do such studies and research on a regular basis and yet they are still very careful every time they make an investment. Be very keen on doing research. The more that you research and understand ether the more easily you can predict its price movement.

- **Buy & Hold**

This is probably the simplest and very effective strategy that you would love to learn when you invest in ether. Indeed, many real-life success stories are based on this strategy. Its power lies in its simplicity. As the name suggests, it is about buying ether and then holding on to it for some time. The idea here is to wait for its price to increase. You can then sell it at a profit at some future date. Take note that you cannot just apply this strategy at any time that you want. The proper way of using this approach is to first study the cryptocurrency concerned, ether. You should apply the buy and hold strategy only if it appears that the price of ether is most likely going to increase. Hence, when you think that the price is most likely going to surge higher and higher, then it is time to use this strategy. However, if after doing your research, you realize that the price of ether is most likely going to drop, then do not use this strategy. Another important part to take note of is when to sell your ether at a profit. Do not underestimate how highly volatile ether is. Sometimes holding on to your ether for too long may not be a good idea. To be sure, you need to keep a close eye on the market and continue to study Ethereum, so that you will know if you should still continue to hold on to your investment or if it time for you to sell it at a profit. Also, before you sell your ether, remember that there is a difference between the buy price and the sell price. The buy price is always higher than the sell price. This is also how a trading broker makes money. Consider the difference and make sure that you sell at a profit.

- **Only invest the money that you can afford to lose**

A common advice that is given to casino gamblers is to gamble only with the money that they can afford to lose. Although investing in ether is not gambling, the same advice still applies. After all, no matter how much you research and study the market, you can only increase your chances of making the right investment decision, but you cannot guarantee the return of positive profit. Hence, you should only invest the money that you can afford to lose. Just like any other investment, investing in ether or any other cryptocurrency has its risks. Therefore, do not invest using the money that you need to pay for your household bills and other obligations. This is also a good way to prevent you from trading under pressure. When you are pressured, your emotions may cloud your judgment which will prevent you from thinking objectively. When you deal with the cryptocurrency market, it is important that you can think clearly and decide objectively.

- **Join online groups and forums**

You should join and participate in online groups and forums on cryptocurrencies. This is a good way for you not only to meet people with a similar interest but you can also learn interesting views and strategies from them. Many cryptocurrency developers are also active in such places, so this is a good way for you to gain valuable information.

- **Learn about other cryptocurrencies**

Although your main interest is investing in Ethereum, it is still important for you to keep an open mind and learn about other cryptocurrencies. Do not forget that Ethereum is not the only profitable cryptocurrency in the market. Also, these other cryptocurrencies also affect how ether performs in the market since they are in competition with one another. By studying and learning about other cryptocurrencies, you will be more able to understand why ether behaves in a certain way.

- **Learn to wait**

Sometimes the market can be difficult to predict despite the amount of research that you do. Indeed, even in the past, the price of Ethereum also experienced some instability. Although it has already gained popularity and established itself in the market today, it does not mean that it will no longer face any problem. A common mistake committed by many investors and traders is to enter a position even when they are not confident enough if it would turn out to be profitable or not. You should keep in mind that you should only invest in ether if you are convinced based on your research that its price is most likely going to increase. If you are not that confident that it will be profitable, then learn to just wait it out. It is common for ether to be hard to predict. However, there are also moments when you are almost 100% certain of its price movement. You can then take advantage of such momentous occasions to make a profit. Be patient and always observe proper timing. Do not forget that you are not in any way compelled to make any investment. But, when you see that ether is getting the best of the market, then be sure that you are there to take full advantage of it.

- **Have fun**

Enjoy it. Enjoy the perks of being an investor. You can also think more clearly and be a more effective investor/trader if you are having fun. Of course, do not confuse this with making reckless decisions and investments. To have fun means to enjoy the process and the life of being a cryptocurrency investor. Hence, enjoy the process of doing research on Ethereum, as well as other cryptocurrencies. If you want, you might want to team up with a friend or simply another investor who is interested in Ethereum. Also, do not take it too seriously. Sometimes being too serious can hinder your creative mind from harnessing its power and coming up with interesting and profitable ideas. So, enjoy and have fun, yet stay professional.

CHAPTER 8:
THE MINING PROCESS OF ETHER

For every block of records or transactions, miners rely on the use of computers to quickly and repeatedly find answers to the puzzle until one of the miners get the right answer to the problem. More specifically, the process is like this: Miners will use the unique header metadata of a block, which includes the timestamp and software version. This is made using a hash function. This will return with a string of random-looking numbers and letters, changing the "nonce value," which affects the hash value.

If a miner finds a hash that matches with the target, then the miner will be awarded ether. This will broadcast the block to the whole network which has the effect of being validated by every node and added to the blockchain as an immutable and verified record. The miners are like racing with one another in such a way that if another miner finds the right hash for the current target, then the other miners will move on and mine another block.

This solving method is what is referred to as "proof of work." It is impossible for any miner to cheat since there is no way that a miner can fake solving a block. There is always a need for a miner to find the right answer to the "puzzle." Once the right hash is identified, verification will come quickly and seamlessly, and this will take place in every node of the blockchain network.

Records show that it takes miners around 12 to 15 seconds to find and solve a block. The Ethereum algorithm adjusts the difficulty of the problem depending on the how fast or slow the miners get to solve the problem so that miners can solve the blocks within the said approximate period. It is also important for blocks to be hard to crack since it protects the transaction. It is a normal part of cryptography whereby legible information is converted to hard-to-crack codes.

The miners earn ether at random. The amount of profit that they earn depends primarily on luck, as well as the amount of computing power they use of mining ether.

Ethereum uses *ethash* as its proof-of-work algorithm. It is designed in such a way that mining would require more memory, which makes mining more difficult, if not impossible, if using ASIC. However, as already noted, Ethereum is about to transition to Casper, which will make mining ether a lot easier.

CHAPTER 9:
SHOULD I INVEST IN ETHER?

Ethereum is one of the most popular and successful cryptocurrencies in the world. Does this also mean that it is a profitable investment? To give you an idea: Had you invested in Ethereum last year (2017), then you would have experienced a profit of over 13,000%. So, is it profitable? *Definitely, yes.* Instead of investing in stocks where an annual profit of 25% is already considered high, you may have to reconsider what the word *high* means when you invest in Ethereum. In 2017, the price of Ethereum increased by 32% in just a 24-hour timeline. This is one of the best things about investing in Ethereum. Just like other cryptocurrencies, it has a high volatility. However, unlike other cryptocurrencies in the market today, the price of Ethereum has been increasing consistently over time. Of course, it is also subject to the usual fluctuations in the market as faced by all other cryptocurrencies, but if you take a closer look and examine its long-term trend, it is easy to say that Ethereum is definitely on the rise.

Just like other cryptocurrencies, Ethereum also has a high volatility. This means that certain risks can be expected. Just like investing in bitcoin or any other cryptocurrency, there is no 100% guarantee that investing in Ethereum will be profitable. There was a time when some people thought that Ethereum would no longer survive in the market when its price dropped considerably. However, as can be expected from a cryptocurrency that has a strong value, Ethereum was able to recover and even turned out to be more profitable than ever.

Today, more and more people are investing in Ethereum which also explains why the price of Ethereum has been constantly increasing. Not to mention, many altcoins use the Ethereum blockchain platform as the base foundation of their own cryptocurrency. As such, there is a high and growing demand for Ethereum. Ethereum is not just any other cryptocurrency. It promotes the use of smart contracts and distributed applications, which are both viewed as highly valuable and useful by the market.

When you invest in Ethereum, you can earn as little and as high as you want. Many experts expect that the price of Ethereum will further increase this 2018, especially considering the fact that it was only in the latter part of 2017 when Ethereum has hit the mainstream and attracted the attention of the big part of the cryptocurrency market.

So, why Ethereum? After all, there are so many other cryptocurrencies in the market. Answer: Because of all other cryptocurrencies out there, including bitcoin, Ethereum appears to be the one that is highly profitable. All that you need to do is to examine the past and present trend of Ethereum, and you will see for yourself just how profitable it is. Facts also suggest that this 2018 is most likely the year when Ethereum is going to hit it really big in the market. Still, the developers of Ethereum has to do their job and keep the system well functioning and at par with its competitors. As an investor, it is your job to keep a close eye on the market, especially on Ethereum, to ensure that your investment will stay in a profitable position. Whether you invest in ether or not is up to you. The best suggestion would be for you to make your own fundamental analysis of this cryptocurrency and decide for yourself if this is the investment opportunity that you are willing to take. Just like when investing in any other cryptocurrency, there is always the possibility that you might lose your investment, but there is also the great possibility that you may earn a high amount of profit. To recall, in 2017, the price of ether surged as high as 13,000%.

CHAPTER 10:
THE FUTURE OF ETHEREUM

Although this book does not promote Ethereum in any way but merely shares the facts about it, it can be said that the future of Ethereum, especially this 2018, looks bright for Ethereum. All you need to do is to check and analyze the past and current trend, be updated on the news about Ethereum, and you will easily see for yourself just how profitable investing in Ethereum can be. Unlike bitcoin, Ethereum creates limitless possibilities since you can build applications and utilities on top of the Ethereum blockchain. With the use of smart contracts and distributed applications, the possibilities are almost infinite.

This 2018 is also the year that experts say that the *flippening* will most likely happen. What is this flippening? It refers to the time when Ethereum will finally overtake bitcoin and become known as the number one cryptocurrency in the world. Although there is no 100% certainty that this will indeed occur, it is a fact that among the cryptocurrencies in the market, Ethereum is the one in the best position that can make this happen. Just to be clear, there is no guarantee that Ethereum will win over bitcoin this year or in the future, but there is a good possibility for this to take place. Hence, you should really keep a close eye on Ethereum.

While Bitcoin promotes itself as a mere cryptocurrency and payment processor that seem to take the place of banks and also get in competition with fiat money (which can alert governments and compel them to issue and impose strict regulations), Ethereum avoids antagonism. Instead, it offers not just the possibility of using a cryptocurrency that can be used for transactions or medium of exchange, but it primarily promotes the use of its blockchain which allows its users the use of smart contracts and distributed applications.

As already discussed, Ethereum has many possible uses. It is expected that in the future, more and more individuals and businesses will make use of the Ethereum blockchain as the base foundation of their own technology. Indeed, developers will find value in using the Ethereum blockchain. Ethereum is still considered a young technology of itself; hence, it is expected that as it continues to grow and mature, more and more enhancements will be made, and the market will see it as more valuable than it is at the present moment.

As for the price of Ethereum, it is most likely that it will increase significantly in the future. If you think that the 13,000% increase that it experienced in 2017 can no longer be repeated, then you should reconsider your opinion as Ethereum takes the market lead and completely dominate the whole cryptocurrency market.

www.ingramcontent.com/pod-product-compliance
Lightning Source LLC
Chambersburg PA
CBHW070203230526
45471CB00002B/795